T0193580

HOMELESS AL

A Little Boy's Story

DELESIA ROBINSON

Al lives in Cleveland with his mom and Oscar the fish. They are forced to leave their home and move into a homeless shelter. Through the difficult times, Al and his mom hold on to their faith in God. When winter and the New Year arrive, nice people begin to give. Al and his mom now have a new place to live. The author places biblical scripture throughout the manuscript to show how faith can help one get through the best and worst times.

Dedicated to Nathaniel Bryce, Mona Kaye, and Carmen Lynn.
Special thanks to Danielle A. Thomas, and Angela Hill for their insight.
In Loving memory of Lular Marie Warren.

MY name is AL.

Before I formed thee in the belly I knew thee; and before thou camest forth out of the womb I sanctified thee, [and] I ordained thee a prophet unto the nations. **Jeremiah 1:5 (KJV)**

Oscar *the fish is my pal.*

"Again, the kingdom from heaven is like a large net thrown into the sea that gathered all kinds of fish. **Matthew 13:47 (ISV)**

Our home was on 1234 Snow Road in Cleveland Ohio.

One day we had to go.

In all our ways acknowledge Him and He will direct our paths. **Proverbs 3:6 (AKJV)**

My mom said, "Oh no!!!"

Have mercy on me, O Lord, for I call to you all day long. **Psalm 86:3 NIV**

Now we live in a shelter.

For I was hungry and you gave me something to eat, I was thirsty and you gave me something to drink, I was a stranger and you invited me in, **Matthew 25:35 NIV**

We are in by six.

We are out by nine.

Oscar and I make it to school

just in time.

Study to show yourself approved to God, a workman that needs not to be ashamed, rightly dividing the word of truth. **2Timothy 2:15 (AKJV)**

Time passes by.
To every thing there is a season, and a time to every purpose under the heaven. ***Ecclesiastes 3:1 (KJV)***

Winter is here.

Perhaps I will stay with you awhile, or even spend the winter, so that you can help me on my journey, wherever I go **1Corithians 16:6 (NIV)**

It's a New Year.

You crown the year with your bounty, and your carts overflow with abundance **Psalm 65:11 (NIV)**

Nice people give.

Dear friends, since God so loved us, we also ought to love one another. **1 John 4:11 NIV**

We have a new place to live.

In my Father's house are many mansions: if it were not so, I would have told you. I go to prepare a place for you. ***John 14:2 (KJV)***

My name is AL.

He counts the stars and calls them all by name. **Psalm 147:4 (NLT)**

THE END.

Train up a child in the way he should go: and when he is old, he will not depart from it. **Proverbs 22:6 (KJV)**

Statistics

Ohio *(OH)*

Total People Experiencing Homelessness on a Given Night in 2015

Total Homeless Population	11,182
Persons in Families Experiencing Homelessness	3,617
Veterans Experiencing Homelessness	1,183
Persons Experiencing Chronic Homelessness	1,275
Unaccompanied Young Adults (Aged 18-24) Experiencing Homelessness	721
Rate of Homelessness per 100,000 Population	96

Resource: https://www.usich.gov/tools-for-action/map/

Community Resources in Cleveland, Ohio

Community Service Alliance
Main address is 4001 Trent Ave.
Cleveland, Ohio 44109
Telephone number is (216) 939-0610
The non-profit provides low rent, affordable housing to people transitioning from homelessness and there is also support for ex-offenders. If they can't assist, then the site may also provide referrals to other shelters and housing programs in the community. Employment assistance services are also available.

Continue Life
Address: 17917 Euclid Ave.
Cleveland, OH 44112
Call (216) 383-1984 for intake.
This is for women and single parents. It coordinates longer-term housing. While the resident stays there they will work towards moving to permanent housing.

Emmanuel Promise Of Hope Ministries
Cleveland, OH 44103
(216) 391-5766
Rooms are available for people moving from homelessness to self-sufficiency.

Family Promise Of Greater Cleveland
Location is 3470 E 152nd St., Cleveland, OH 44110, Telephone number is (216) 767-4060 or 2592 W 14th St., Cleveland, Ohio 44113, dial (216) 751-7301
Services are offered to help move people from a short term home, shelter or apartment into a permanent unit in Cuyahoga County. Get information on, and apply for programs such as funds for deposits and other needs.

North Point Transitional Housing Center

Main location is 1550 Superior Ave.

Cleveland, Ohio 44114

(216) 455-0095

Provides transitional housing for homeless residents and men who are able to work and have an income.

St. Herman's House of Hospitality

4410 Franklin Blvd.

Cleveland, Ohio 44113

Community Resources in Cleveland, Ohio

West Haven Youth Shelter

Address is 3020 W 104th St

Cleveland, OH 44111

Call (216) 941-0063

Northcoast Behavioral Healthcare - E 118th St. Residential Site

Main address is 1502 E 118th St.

Cleveland, OH 44106

For intake, dial (216) 661-2411

Short-term emergency housing is offered for mentally ill, homeless adults in the community.

Oriana House

Location is 1804 E 55th St.

Cleveland, Ohio 44103

(216) 881-7882

Temporary housing to offenders who are determined to be low risk. Residents will be required to attend case management, seek employment and find permanent housing.

Salvation Army Of Greater Cleveland, Harbor Light Complex

Social services, an emergency shelter, food, financial aid, and more is provided to seniors, veterans, and the less fortunate. This is an option for employed men whose goal is to save money and become self-sufficient. Utilities, free meals, and more is provided, such as clothing.

- 1710 Prospect Ave., Cleveland, Ohio 44115, (216) 781-3773
- 2501 E 22nd St., Cleveland, OH 44115, (216) 623-7492

Transitional Housing

Location is 1545 W 25th St.
Cleveland, Ohio 44113
Main phone - (216) 781-2250
Affordable housing for women and single parents in order to help people become self-sufficient.

2100 Lakeside Men's Homeless Shelter

Cleveland, OH

Haven House For Veterans

3468 E 142nd St.
Cleveland, OH 44120
Phone Number: 216-491-4730

Community Resources in Cleveland, Ohio
Volunteers Of America Of Greater Ohio

A transitional shelter for homeless men. Housing and case management is offered for homeless veterans. Also, get information on short and long term shelter, government benefits, and other housing services.

-2710 Walton Ave., Cleveland, Ohio 44113, (216) 621-0120
-775 E 152nd St., Cleveland, OH 44110, (216) 541-9000

The City Mission Men's Crisis Center
Main location is 5310 Carnegie Ave
Cleveland, OH 44103
Call (216) 431-3510

West Side Catholic Center - Women And Children's Shelter
Cleveland, OH 44113
(216) 631-4141
The non-profit, charity provides longer-term housing and it is designed to move residents to permanent housing. Get information on financial aid, case management, meals, and clothing. Numerous social services are offered to the poor and low income.

YMCA Of Greater Cleveland - Y-haven
Main address is 6001 Woodland Ave. 6th Floor
Cleveland, OH 44104
Telephone number is (216) 431-2018

Or call 211(United Way Greater Cleveland)

National Resources

Homelessness | HHS.gov

http://www.hhs.gov/programs/social-services/homelessness/ind...

Links to studies, publications, local resources in your community, US Department of Health and Human Services **resources** and other web sites.

Runaway & Homeless Youth | Family and Youth...

http://www.acf.hhs.gov/programs/fysb/programs/**runaway**-homele... Call 1-800-**RUNAWAY** if you are thinking of running from home

Domestic Trafficking Hotlines - US Department of...

http://www.state.gov/j/tip/id/domestic/
Call the National Human Trafficking Resource Center at 1-888-373-7888

The Salvation Army

http://www.salvationarmyusa.org/

Habitat For Humanity Is Changing Lives With Homes

www.**Habitat**.org

Intended for School age children. Churches and Christians, Christian book stores, Literacy programs, Sunday School classes, Social Justice forums etc.

"Homeless AL is a way to open up dialogue with parents and children about less fortunate families, and applying biblical principles to daily life."

Delesia Robinson was born and raised in East Cleveland, Ohio. She is currently living in Midtown Cleveland with her husband Darryl. Delesia started her career as a Registered nurse at St. Lukes Medical center in 1986. In July of 2013, Delesia founded an organization called Pride Among Daughters & Sisters, aka PADS. PADS is a 501c3 geared toward empowering and educating underprivileged girls and women while making costly feminine hygiene products available. She developed a relationship with the Hunger Network of Greater Cleveland's Stay Well Program in 2014, and has done events with them on Cleveland's East and West side. In 2015 Delesia was nominated for the American Jewish Committee's(AJC) Isaiah Award for Human relations. The award is given to local non profits to lead the way in building a better and more just society. You can contact Delesia Robinson at www.prideamongdaughters.org.

About the Artist

Khadijah Raheem is a talented young artist. She is a graduate of Shaw high school in East Cleveland, Ohio. She is a 21 year old single mom. Her daughter's name is Isabella.

A portion of the proceeds of Homeless AI will go to the public charity Pride Among Daughters and Sisters aka PADS. Our mission is to provide sanitary pads, tampons, and feminine hygiene products(incontinence products, menstrual cups, wipes) and the education that goes with it to underserved girls, and women to promote pride, dignity and confidence.

WestBow Press books may be ordered through booksellers or by contacting:

WestBow Press
A Division of Thomas Nelson & Zondervan
1663 Liberty Drive
Bloomington, IN 47403
www.westbowpress.com
1 (866) 928-1240

Because of the dynamic nature of the Internet, any web addresses or links contained in this book may have changed since publication and may no longer be valid. The views expressed in this work are solely those of the author and do not necessarily reflect the views of the publisher, and the publisher hereby disclaims any responsibility for them.

Any people depicted in stock imagery provided by Thinkstock are models, and such images are being used for illustrative purposes only. Certain stock imagery © Thinkstock.

ISBN: 978-1-5127-4926-7 (sc)
ISBN: 978-1-5127-4927-4 (e)

Library of Congress Control Number: 2016911065

Print information available on the last page.

WestBow Press rev. date: 07/20/2016

WESTBOW
PRESS®
A DIVISION OF THOMAS NELSON
& ZONDERVAN

Printed in the United States
By Bookmasters